THE IRONBRIDGE GORGE

Introduction

'… a precipitate descent to the Romantic scene of Colebrook Dale, where the river, winding between a variety of high, wooded hills, is crossed by a bridge of one arch 100ft [30.5m] in length and formed entirely of cast iron with strong, stone abutments … a striking effect in landscape and a stupendous specimen of the powers of mechanism.'

HENRY SKINE, 1798

The deep valley now known as the Ironbridge Gorge was created some 15,000 years ago at the end of the Ice Age. A strong, raging torrent of water was forced to change direction by a glacier which blocked its way. In doing so, it cut through the limestone mass of Wenlock Edge, creating a deep chasm and exposing the layers of raw materials which were later to be the making of the valley's fortunes: limestone, iron ore, coals and clays.

The Ironbridge Gorge Museums are spread across this unique river gorge and seek to bring alive the events that happened here over many centuries – events that changed all our lives.

In the old Severn Warehouse, an intricate model of the Ironbridge Gorge as it was in 1796 displays the whole valley from Dale End to the eastern end of the Gorge beyond Coalport. The contents of this model took many

PANEL 1: *The area which is now Blists Hill was a thriving industrial site in the eighteenth and nineteenth centuries, full of coal and clay mines, rail and plateways, canals and ironworks, brick and tileworks. The Blists Hill blast furnaces were busy from the 1830s onwards and now form part of the 'archaeological corridor' of Blists Hill, along with other original features like the Shropshire Canal and the partially restored Brick and Tile Works, which used to extend over a vast area of the site.*

In 1796 the Coalport China works was still in its infancy, and the revolutionary Hay Inclined Plane, designed to transport canal boats between the different levels of the Shropshire Canal, was brand new.

PANEL 2: *To the east of Blists Hill and along the river were an early huddle of potteries and mines, forges and foundries, which had grown up rapidly in response to the success of the Coalbrookdale ironworks. On the south side of the river, the early industrial settlement of Broseley was thriving, known for its clay products and tobacco pipes. Cannon foundries, smelters and boat yards were all busy along the southern bank.*

It was to be another half-century or so before the famous decorative tile industry came into its own in Jackfield, also on the southern side. The two largest factories in the world would be sited here, and today the Jackfield Tile Museum is housed in the former Craven Dunnill Tile Works. Bedlam Furnaces, the location for Philip de Loutherbourg's celebrated painting Coalbrookdale by Night *of 1801 are on the northern riverbank.*

years to research and six months to construct. It represents a particular day in the history of Coalbrookdale – by which name it was long known before the name of Ironbridge became predominant – 12 August 1796 when the Prince of Orange, Stadtholder Willem V, and his wife Wilhelmina visited the many industries of the Gorge.

The model shows many of the areas now occupied by the current Museums and helps to orientate the visitor.

RIGHT: *Enjoying the view as it was in 1796*

PANEL 3: *The great symbol of the success of the iron industry was the Iron Bridge. Cast in 1779 by Abraham Darby III, its great arch enthralled visitors who came from all over the world to admire its construction. In 1796 the stone abutments on the south side were still in place, although already cracking. The dense river traffic – trows which plied the ports of the Severn carrying the raw materials of industry, and ferries which carried its workforce – made the river a motorway of its day.*

The Tontine Hotel, on the northern end of the Bridge was built in 1784 and by 1796 had already expanded to cope with increased trade. The Market Square was constructed and the market moved from Madeley to the brash new upstart town soon to be known as Ironbridge.

PANEL 4: *The building in which the Museum of the River now stands, the former Severn Warehouse, has yet to be built but it is easy to locate the wharf onto which the royal party is disembarking. Opposite is the Bower Yard, well known for boatbuilding, and up the hill is the lead-smelter often pictured in the early paintings of the Iron Bridge. This far end of the Gorge is closest to the historic heart of Coalbrookdale where the earliest iron-smelting with coke, instead of charcoal, took place. Abraham Darby I, a Quaker ironmaster who had moved here from his Bristol brass foundry, began this successful transition from the old to the new technology in 1709. As a result the iron industry in Coalbrookdale was to become a world leader.*

The Ironbridge Gorge

The valley running north from the River Severn at the western end of the Gorge is known today as Coalbrookdale. Over 200 years ago, the whole area was known by this name. Many of the original features so fundamental to the success of the early iron industry here are now hidden or have not survived. Yet it is still possible to understand the important events of this valley and to visit many of the places in which they happened.

RIGHT: Tapping iron from the furnace; a reconstruction in the Museum of Iron

BELOW: Dale House completed 1717

In 1708 Abraham Darby I, a Quaker brass-founder, whose family originated in the Black Country, left Bristol and settled in Coalbrookdale. He leased the old charcoal furnace from Sir Basil Brooke, lord of the manor, and in 1709 finally succeeded in smelting iron with cheap and plentiful coke instead of expensive charcoal. Cutting down large areas of woodland to produce charcoal was having a serious effect on the country's economy, and many ironmasters elsewhere had tried but failed to use coal as fuel for ironmaking. It is recorded that Darby bought a special consignment of beer for his men, obviously recognising his success as significant.

He intended to make cheap iron pots and other domestic items. In doing so he started a dynasty of iron-founders who were in no small way to change the face of industry.

The Darby family built a number of houses close to the ironworks. Today part of Dale House is open to visitors, who may see the study in which Darby's grandson planned the construction of the world's first great Iron Bridge.

Adjacent is the house Rosehill, restored and filled with many of the possessions of the Darbys and their relatives. It shows the house as it would have been in the 1850s.

ABOVE: Hannah Mary, daughter of Richard and Rebecca Reynolds and cousin of Abraham Darby III, married William Rathbone, of the Liverpool Quaker family. His 1780s' suit with brilliant cut steel buttons is in the Museum's costume collection

ABOVE: *The Long Warehouse and, on the right, the Great Warehouse, which is now the Museum of Iron*

'A new way of casting iron bellied potts ... in sand only, without loam or clay by which iron potts ... may be cast fine ... and with more ease and expedition and in regard to their cheapnesse may be of great advantage to the poore of this kingdome, who for the most part use such ware ... and likewise may in time supply foreign markets with that manufacture of our own dominions ...'

INTRODUCTION TO
DARBY'S PATENT
OF 1707

ABOVE: *The earliest known engraving of Coalbrookdale, made by François Vivares in 1758. It shows an ironmaster leaning on the railing close to the Darby Furnace and pointing to a cast-iron steam engine cylinder being transported. No portraits of the first three Abraham Darbys exist, but perhaps the ironmaster is Abraham II, who took over from his father and made vast improvements to the company's operation*

RIGHT: *Cast-iron cooking-pots were exported from Coalbrookdale to all parts of the world*

In the years following the death of Abraham I, the Coalbrookdale ironworks became well known. Abraham II concentrated on perfecting the forging of wrought-iron using coke, and other furnaces were built to cope with increasing demand.

Artists came to paint and sketch the revolutionary scenes of life, landscape and industry within the Gorge.

Yet for many working in the ironworks or in the coalmines, life went on much as before in some respects. Small-holdings and livestock were kept, vegetables grown and beer brewed. Eighteenth-century company houses were built for the workforce at the same time as some families were building 'squatter' settlements, many of which survived well into the twentieth century.

BELOW: *Holywell Lane, Little Dawley – a late eighteenth-century squatter settlement, which survived until the 1960s*

RIGHT: *View down the Coalbrookdale valley towards the River Severn, painted by William Williams in 1777:* Morning View

ABOVE: *Carpenters Row, 1780 terrace built by the Coalbrookdale Company for its workforce. Rent was 9½d in 1794*

At Blists Hill a re-erected squatter cottage vividly illustrates the lifestyle of the ordinary labourer of the valley.

A contemporary account of Coalbrookdale, three years before the Iron Bridge was built, paints an atmospheric picture:

'The old furnace (nearest the house) has been in blast without the least diminution for 7 years last past. It continues to vomit out its flames and emit a vast Column of Smoak. The great number of Buildings for the Furnaces, Forges, Founderies, Warehouses etc and the habitations of the Workmen, 200 of whom are imployed, compose a little City …'
J.M. FISHER'S *TRAVEL JOURNAL OF 1776*

In the next century, John Randall wrote of widespread cholera caused by poor living conditions:

'… so far as our knowledge and experience served us we should say that the first victims in this neighbourhood were among men and women who led irregular lives, and who lived in dirty ill-ventilated homes and in the decks and cabins of the barges ... in which men slept and ate … and who drank the polluted water of the river.'

'At Madeley, girls, whose average age will be eighteen years (though several quite old and middle aged women are numbered amongst them) work on the pit mounds … they have to be on the pit-banks at 6.00 am … and receive from 8d to 1/- a day …'
ADA NIELD, *FROM SCOTLAND TO SALOP*, 1897

When the Prince and Princess of Orange visited Ironbridge in 1796, they visited Coalport – or 'Coalpark' as it was written in one of the newspaper reports of the day – where 'Her Royal Highness bought some pieces of Mr Rose'.

In this year John Rose set up a new china works close to the site of the present Coalport China Museum; he had previously had a china works on the south bank of the Severn. He was only twenty-four, and his partner and presumably backer was a local industrialist, Edward Blakeway, who was also a shareholder in the Iron Bridge.

The young Rose would have been delighted to show off his finest wares to the royal family from the Low Countries.

In the next century Coalport was to become one of the largest porcelain producers in the world. It exported its wares overseas, and its markets included most of the crowned heads of Europe.

Much of Coalport's work-force came by ferry from the settlement of Jackfield on the south side of the river, and many were women, who often worked as burnishers and tranferrers.

John Rose was one of the first manufacturers to introduce lead-free glazes, as early as 1820, in an attempt to limit the disease known as potters' rot. Astonishingly, it was not until the 1950s that lead-free glazes became compulsory in the industry.

The present-day beautiful riverside setting of Coalport belies its earlier history as a 'new town' of the 1790s. Coal-fired kilns, tar-boiling and the burning of bones being prepared for use in the china works must have made it a very unpleasant place. Today, a youth hostel is housed in the 'John Rose' building, the earliest surviving structure on the site, which was principally used as a decorating shop for the works.

ABOVE: *Ferries regularly crossed the river between Jackfield and Coalport transporting the workforce, and trows plied the length of the Severn carrying iron, coal and clay until the 1880s*

LEFT: *John Rose may have personally shown his products to the Prince and Princess of Orange. The records do not say, but costume and pictorial research as well as knowledge of his earliest products provide some clues*

ABOVE: *Coalport China Museum from the south bank of the Severn*

RIGHT: *One of the earliest Coalport factory products on display in the Museum: a 1796 jug*

diameter is likewise of Cast Iron. But all these are trifling compared with the great Tools for which they have occasion in the progress of their Business. Their Boilers and Cylinders, and above all, their Conduits for water to turn the Mills which they serve instead of Races, and answer much better, as less Water is wasted both by the exhalation of the Sun, and what the ground would absorb. All these are of Cast Iron ...

'Their Water wheels are likewise composed of Iron. The Crank of the Great Wheel which sets the Bellows to work weighs 50 cwt

ABOVE: *Philip de Loutherbourg's* Coalbrookdale by Night, *1801*

RIGHT: *Pouring hot iron in the foundry at Blists Hill*

An eighteenth-century description conveys the vast array of uses for cast-iron:

'It is astonishing to think of the uses to which Cast Iron is converted. Besides common castings, they make Chimney Tops, their window Cases, their Chimney Pieces, their sashes, their floors, their Scantlen for their Roofs, Doors, Pallisadoes, Ploughshares, besides an hundred other Utensils for domestic Use of this permanent and durable material. The Arch over one of their Door Cases which is 16ft [4.9m] in

[2.5 tonnes]. The axes weigh 140 cwt [7.1 tonnes] and besides this the whole Wheel is of Iron, even the Ladles and shroudings. The diameter of this Wheel is about 25 feet [7.6m] … and there are to this Bellows three large Cylinders 78 inches [2m] in diameter. The bellows rise 4 feet [1.2m] at a time. While one is up the other falls so air is constantly gushing through the Funnel with equal Force … It is impossible to conceive with what vehemence the Air rushes into the Furnace or the roaring which it occasions …'
J.M. FISHER, 1776

This account portrays a vivid and even horrific picture of what it must have been like to live, breathe and work in this, the most industrialised place on earth in the late eighteenth century.

RIGHT: Blowing engine in the north engine house of the Blists Hill blast furnaces

LEFT: A typical fireplace surround produced by the Coalbrookdale Company in the nineteenth century

ABOVE: Blists Hill blast furnaces built in the 1830s and '40s and painted by Warrington Smyth in 1847

RIGHT: Blists Hill furnaces at work in the late nineteenth century. They ceased working in 1912

Coalport

In the seventeenth and early eighteenth centuries the area now known as the Ironbridge Gorge was full of small potteries working with local clays.

On the south side of the River Severn, Broseley was famous for its clay products, especially its tobacco pipes, which had been made there since at least the early 1600s. It was on this same side of the river that many of the more well-known potteries flourished, even into the nineteenth century.

In 1772 Thomas Turner arrived at the Caughley china works and began producing porcelain. He had previously worked at Worcester. The well-known 'blue and white' Caughley ware copied the vogue for oriental patterns and colours. Caughley, and later Coalport, made porcelain from Cornish, not local clays.

The real impetus for the success of Coalport as a 'new town' came from the inventive genius of William Reynolds, cousin of Abraham Darby III, the builder of the Iron Bridge.

ABOVE RIGHT: *William Reynolds, 'liberal promoter of the different Arts and sciences … to whom the Nation at large stands greatly indebted'*

RIGHT: *Caughley ware asparagus set displayed in the Alfred Darby Gallery, Coalport China Museum*

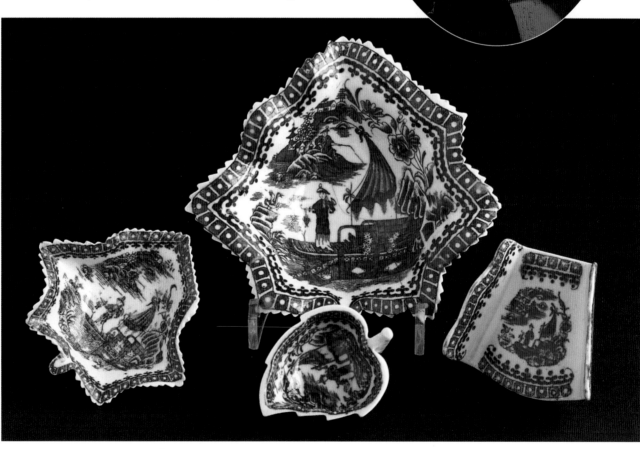

William Reynolds was often considered 'the ablest and most imaginative of the eighteenth century Shropshire ironmasters'.

'Coalport, being the termination of the Shropshire Canal. Here is an Inclin'd Plane 960ft [292.6m] long falling 7¾ inches per yard [216mm per metre] for the Conveyance of boats up and down a high hill, the business being perform'd much quicker than by locks …

'Near this is a long subterraneous passage from whence great quantities of Coal is brought and within which is a spring of petroleum or fossil tar …

'… along a road by the side of the Canal … an Excellent China Manufactory belonging to Blakeway & Rose, and tho' erected but a few years, the goods manufactored here are supposed to excel any other in the Nation …'

H. GRAHAM, *COALBROOKDALE*, 1801

The Hay Inclined Plane was revolutionary when it opened in 1792. It dramatically reduced the travelling time of canal tub-boats by traditional locks from several hours to minutes. The decline of the canals meant that it fell into disuse, and it was officially abandoned in 1907.

The Tar Tunnel was cut in 1786 in an attempt to give the Blists Hill mines direct access to the Severn. The natural bitumen which flowed forth provided good revenues for Reynolds for a time – and still oozes today.

TOP: *The cast-iron Coalport Bridge of 1818 replaced a wooden bridge of 1780*

LEFT: *The Hay Inclined Plane, now within Blists Hill Open Air Museum, allowed a pair of tub-boats to pass from one level of the Shropshire Canal to the other in 3½ minutes*

ABOVE: *The Tar Tunnel extends approximately 1,000yd (900m), and visitors today may don hard hats and go underground for about a tenth of the distance*

The story of Coalport is complex in its beginnings. The Museum occupies some buildings of the china works established about 1800 or later by John Rose's younger brother, Thomas. John Rose eventually took over the whole site around 1815, and his company went on to produce some of the finest work in Europe.

The displays at Coalport ensure that the visitor sees most of the Museum's collections. It is always looking for further examples of Coalport and Caughley wares, and occasionally exciting new

discoveries are made. The Alfred Darby Gallery contains some fine examples of Caughley porcelain. Elsewhere within the Museum is a variety of styles and patterns made by the Coalport factory.

There are spectacular pieces made expressly for exhibitions, commemorative items celebrating coronations and great events, trophies and politicians' pots, as well as exemplary pieces of almost every type of Coalport ware, including miniatures.

Coalport won gold medals and prizes at many international exhibitions, including the

1851 Great Exhibition of All Nations in the Crystal Palace, Hyde Park, along with another great business from the Gorge – the Coalbrookdale Company. However, by the turn of the century trade was declining, and after the First World War wage reductions

LEFT: Sunset at Coalport, overlooking the remains of the Coalport section of the Shropshire Canal, the course of which now lies under the car park

and industrial unrest spelled the end of Coalport by the Severn. The company was sold, and in 1926 the works closed and transferred to Stoke-on-Trent, becoming part of the Wedgwood Group in 1967. Nine years later, with the help of the New Town Corporation of Telford, the Ironbridge Gorge Museum Trust restored the derelict works and re-opened them as Coalport China Museum, winning the first European Museum of the Year Award.

ABOVE: Commemorative plate for the visit to the City of London by the King of Sardinia in 1855

RIGHT: Celebratory archway built to commemorate the visit to the works in 1900 by the Duchess of York, later Queen Mary

MAIN PICTURE: *Many Coalport pieces were made expressly to show off techniques which could produce every conceivable effect. In the foreground is a two-handled tankard depicting the Forest Glen on the slopes of the Wrekin. Today this Victorian tea pavilion has been reconstructed at Blists Hill*

Life for those working in the Coalport China works was not as agreeable as the products it turned out.

The working day at the china works was hard, and a large number of the tasks were arduous for the workforce, many of whom were women. Married women with children were allowed to start a little later for a period of time, but in general the hours were long and there were numerous health risks. Pneumoconiosis – known as potters' rot – was caused by inhaling china clay dust into the lungs and was usually fatal. Burnishing and gilding could cause sores, and lead-poisoning caused by the glazes could result in death.

From all this came the fabulously beautiful: great vases richly painted, pieces of all shapes and colours, jugs with ornate decorative and landscape paintings, and delicate cups and saucers, out of which wealthy Georgians and eminent Victorians would have drunk newly popular tea and coffee.

One china-painter lived throughout the nineteenth century and became famous for his fine bird paintings as well as his longevity. John Randall worked at Coalport for

forty-six years, and many of his pieces can be seen in the Museum. He also wrote histories of the area, ran a local post office and was made a Freeman of the Borough of Wenlock, by which the Ironbridge Gorge

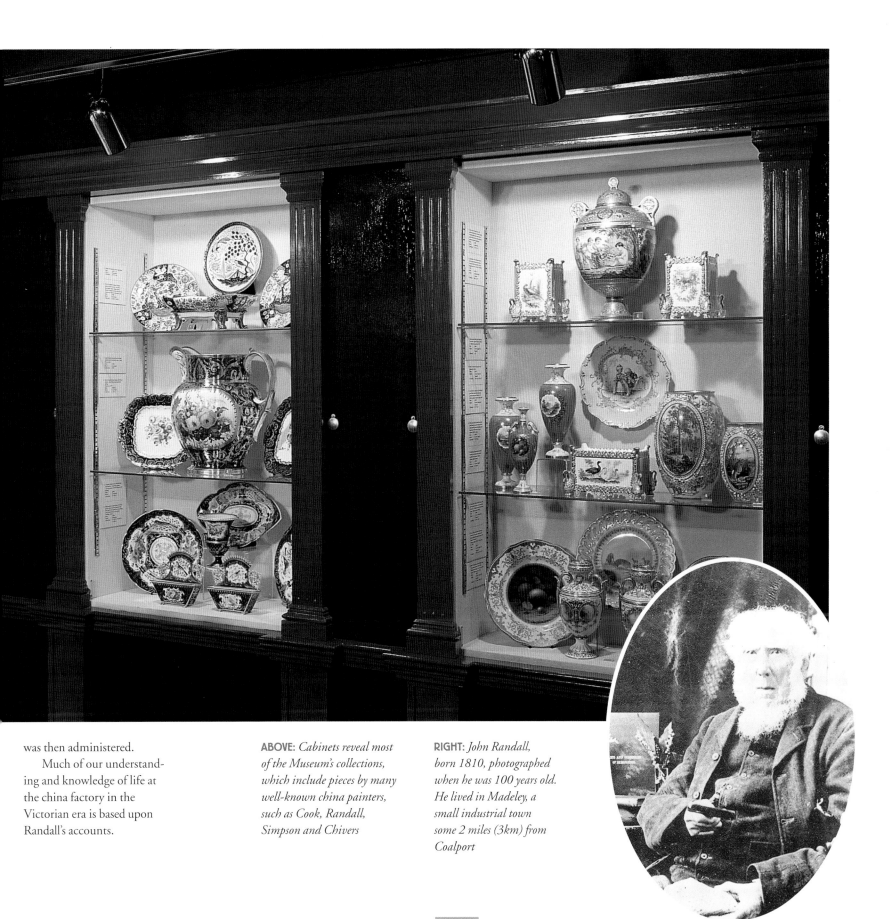

was then administered.

Much of our understanding and knowledge of life at the china factory in the Victorian era is based upon Randall's accounts.

ABOVE: *Cabinets reveal most of the Museum's collections, which include pieces by many well-known china painters, such as Cook, Randall, Simpson and Chivers*

RIGHT: *John Randall, born 1810, photographed when he was 100 years old. He lived in Madeley, a small industrial town some 2 miles (3km) from Coalport*

RIGHT: *Examples of Coalport's Du Barry pink, copied from Sèvres, on show in the Display Kiln. Top row centre is the Pains Lane Racing Trophy*

The Museum has been fortunate to have dedicated volunteers who have tape-recorded the reminiscences of former workers in many of the industries of the Gorge. These provide a rich insight into real life and help the Museum to interpret the artefacts.

'I was born in 1883. I started at Coalport when I was thirteen. I used to cut the prints for the transferrers to put on the china, in the room facing the Coalport Row. As time went on I went into what they call the lower room where I was only on cleaning the china after it came out of the kiln. At the biscuit stage we had to clean it with sandpaper and camel-hair brushes …'
MRS MCKINSEY, A FORMER TRANSFERRER AND POLISHER

'The printing shop consisted of six presses. Each press had two heavy rollers on just like the mangle our mother used to mangle the clothes, only heavier. At each press there was one man who did the pressing of the transfers on metal plates and three women. He used to brush the plates with a kind of size – that is a form of soapy liquid. And then place a piece of paper over it, put it in the press and roll it. And the copper plate came out, and he'd peel the paper off. As he was finishing the sheets for the transfers he would pass them to a young girl – like myself…'
MRS THOMPSON, TRANSFERRER

'… we had to grind the colours till it got them very fine to work on the ware … we had to grind them with a knife, keep grinding it round and round and round. It did make our arms ache but you

LEFT: *An ornate fruit stand, hand-painted by William Cook and dating from 1855. It is marked with the London retailer's name, 'Daniell', as well as 'CBD' for Coalbrookdale*

couldn't use it till you got it proper smooth. Indian Tree would be the first pattern when you went to work for them first. Then you would work yourself up and up until you could do everything

more or less … Mr Simpson was the foreman …'
MRS ADAMS, PAINTRESS

Mrs Adams worked at Coalport in the early twentieth century, at the

same time as Percy Simpson, a splendid Coalport artist and art director whose work can be seen on many pieces in the Museum.

LEFT: *This beautiful baluster-shaped jug is hand-painted by an unknown Coalport artist and dates from 1850*

Coalport became famous for a number of its patterns, many of which were often copied by or from other factories. Some historians of ceramics consider that Coalport was the first china-manufacturer to use the Willow Pattern, and even those with a dislike of ornate porcelain may have a sneaking regard for Indian Tree. It was traditionally believed that this famous design was introduced at Coalport in 1801, yet no piece has ever been found earlier than 1820. The pattern was so popular that at one time a whole section of the factory was devoted to it, and for many years it was the training piece given to all new recruits to the works.

Some 141 other factories all over the country used the Indian Tree design, and a romantic story tells how the pattern was first found on a piece of silk brought back from India by an officer in the King's Shropshire Light Infantry. The exact truth will never be known but the splendid tale is memorable.

Other well-known designs included Ming Rose, Hong Kong and, of course, the Willow Pattern. A whole dinner service was commissioned by a London agent and presented to Tsar Nicholas I by Queen Victoria in 1845. Some of this service remains to this day in the Hermitage Museum in St Petersburg.

Today the Museum runs workshops for both adults and children where visitors may try their hand at making pots, vases and mugs, or small and intricate floral pieces requiring a dexterity which is made to look simple by those demonstating.

ABOVE: *Demonstrators are often to be found in the workshops, slipcasting, painting or decorating wares*

TOP: *Teapot in the Indian Tree pattern*

LEFT: *A blue-ground, 'bat wing' dish. One of the most popular patterns produced by the Coalport company*

ABOVE: *The Jackfield bridge was built in 1994 to replace the 1909 Free Bridge, an early reinforced concrete structure*

RIGHT: *No portraits of the builder of the Iron Bridge exist, but perhaps this is how Abraham Darby III may have reviewed his plans in consultation with his foreman Thomas Gregory (left). John Wilkinson, ironmaster and supporter of Darby, considers the situation shortly after completion of the Bridge*

The Iron Bridge

The area known as Coalbrookdale had been producing iron since the sixteenth century, and coal and limestone were mined from medieval times. The growth of industry after the success of the Darbys meant an increase in population and all its requirements.

In the eighteenth century, the River Severn was the main artery of life for the towns, cities, villages and farms as well as those new and growing industries which lined its banks. Some 400 vessels traded between Gloucester and Welshpool in 1758 and this number doubled within fifty years. In the 1750s, six or more ferry crossings operated within the Severn Gorge, carrying both the raw materials of industry as well as its workforce.

Yet as industry's requirements grew, so did the need for a more permanent and reliable way of crossing the Severn.

In 1773 a Shrewsbury joiner turned architect, Thomas Farnolls Pritchard, wrote to John Wilkinson, a local ironmaster, to suggest a new bridge to be made of cast iron. Wilkinson was a great iron enthusiast and was even nick-named 'Iron Mad' because of his conviction that iron could be used for almost anything. He owned furnaces in Staffordshire and Denbighshire as well as Shropshire. His life was anything but dull, and after his death his vast fortune was consumed in litigation by heirs both legitimate and illegitimate.

Pritchard submitted a design in 1775, and a meeting was held by those prepared to back the new bridge. Darby was commissioned and shares were issued to raise the necessary £3,200 which Darby estimated the Bridge would cost.

In 1776 an Act of Parliament was passed which authorised the new Bridge and prohibited any ferry operating within 500yd (460m) of this revolutionary new structure. Yet in the same year an advertisement appeared seeking tenders to build the Bridge in 'stone, brick or timber' – in fact anything but iron. Doubts would be understandable since iron had never been used before for such a project. Small iron bridges already existed in China, but never of such mass and size.

ABOVE: *A Birmingham enamel snuff-box c1790 inscribed 'A Present from the Iron Bridge', showing that souvenirs are nothing new*

BELOW: *Darby's personal accounts ledger in the Museum Archive shows the real costs and helps to explain how the Iron Bridge was built*

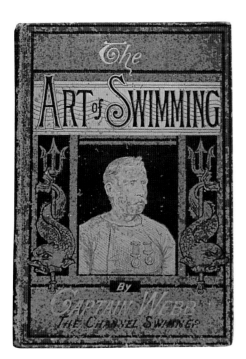

LEFT & BELOW: *Captain Matthew Webb, first cross-Channel swimmer – 1875, trained in the River Severn and rescued his younger brother from drowning there. Many of his medals and other memorabilia are in the Museum's collection*

'The Bridge itself makes a light and elegant appearance tho' apparently no ways deficient in Strength. In viewing it either up or down water it resembles an elegant Arch in some ancient Cathedral …'

Casting the parts for this innovation must have posed considerable challenges to the Coalbrookdale ironworkers. The necessary amount was estimated to be 300 tons [305 tonnes] at £7 a ton, although in the event 378 tons [384 tonnes] were used. Darby had rashly agreed to fund any overspend, which eventually cost him and his Company nearly £3,000. Such a quantity would have taken one furnace three months to produce. The Coalbrookdale Furnace was enlarged in 1777 as shown on the beams bearing Abraham Darby's name, and it seems likely that this was where iron for the Bridge was produced.

Abraham Darby III's team of workmen raised the great arches of the Iron Bridge in the summer of 1779, when the river would have been low and thus would carry little traffic to interfere with their work. To the modern visitor, used to hydraulic cranes and winches, mechanical diggers and metal scaffolding, it is astonishing that it was done at all. Each rib alone weighed 6 tonnes and there must have been an enormous concerted effort on river and land to swing the ribs into position. Despite the fact that extensive records survive from the Darby family, it is perhaps surprising that no detailed account of the actual building of the Bridge exists.

LEFT: The Iron Bridge *by William Williams, 1780*

RIGHT: *The Rogers family, famous for making coracles, have lived in the valley since before the Bridge was built*

ABOVE: *Many of the original eighteenth-century plateway routes that used to bear raw materials to the wharves are now lined with cottages and gardens*

ABOVE RIGHT: *View downstream from the old Severn Warehouse*

RIGHT: *Steep steps from Ironbridge town lead up to St Luke's Church, built in 1837*

BELOW: *Riverside Dale End Park*

TABLE of TOLLS.

For every time they pass over this BRIDGE.

	s d
For every Coach, Landau, Hearse, Chaise, Chair, or such like Carriages drawn by Six Horses, Mares, Geldings, or Mules.	2.0
Ditto ———— by Four Ditto ————	1.6
Ditto ———— by Two Ditto ————	1.0
Ditto ———— by One Ditto ————	0.6
For every Horse, Mule, Ass, pair of Oxen, Drawing or Harness'd to draw any Waggon, Cart, or such like carriage, for each Horse &c	0.3
For a Horse, Mule, or Ass, laden or unladen and not drawing,	0.1½
For a Horse, Mule, or Ass carrying double,	0.2
For an Ox, Cow, or neat cattle	0.1
For a Calf, Pig, Sheep, or lamb	0.0½
For every Horse, Mule, Ass, or carriage going on the roads and not over the Bridge, half the said tolls.	
For every Foot passenger, going over the Bridge	0 0½

N.B. This Bridge being private property, every Officer or Soldier, whether on duty or not, is liable to pay toll for passing over, as well as any baggage waggon, Mail-coach or the Royal Family.

The Iron Bridge opened on New Year's Day 1781. The tolls had already been set in the Act of Parliament and were implemented straight away. Exempt from tolls were those ferry operators who had lost their livelihood, and one might imagine that small children may have skipped over scot-free if they could.

appearing in the ironwork, caused by ground movement. In 1802 the southern stonework was demolished and replaced by wooden arches, which remained there until 1821, when they too were replaced by the iron arches which still stand today.

Traffic continued to cross the Bridge until 1934, when

' … in this strange region we nevertheless noted some of its most remarkable objects, and among them of course the Iron Bridge which was then a great curiosity to me, as I had at that time never seen that at Bridgwater or the other at Sunderland. I think this is the most beautiful of the three, for though it seems like network wrought in iron, it will apparently lay uninjured for ages …' CHARLES DIBDIN, DRAMATIST AND SONGWRITER, AND APPARENTLY A FAVOURITE OF JANE AUSTEN, VISITED THE VALLEY IN 1787.

ABOVE: *The original table of tolls to be paid*

RIGHT: *The Tollhouse keeper in 1921. The furthermost cottage has now gone, along with the railway crossing and the station*

LEFT: *The Severn Warehouse built in the 1830s*

Darby's Quaker beliefs are reflected in the footnote to the table of tolls which plainly states that the military and the royal family were most definitely *not* exempt.

When the Bridge was first built it had stone abutments on both sides as seen in William Williams' painting (see pp. 24–5). However, within a few years cracks were

the road was closed to vehicles, and the tolls were extracted until 1950, when the Rathbone family, related to the Darbys by marriage and who were then the Bridge proprietors, transferred ownership to Shropshire County Council.

In 1972–4 major repairs took place on the foundations of the Bridge. A reinforced-concrete arch was inverted in the bedrock of the river to protect the Bridge from geological pressure. Today English Heritage are the guardians of the Bridge.

'Returning along this path we crossed the road to the second, which is led along the narrow ridge of an eminence agreeably planted with evergreens, which shut out the immense limestone pits to the left hand and interrupt the sight of a deep precipice to the right. This walk terminates with a Rotunda, a most classical building placed at the point of the promontory; whence a view of great extent, diversity and curious combination is unfolded … carrying the eye a little further it takes in the Iron Bridge, the river and its shipping … beyond this it reposes in distant vales and upon the fertile meadows of Shropshire …'

ABOVE: *The view from the Rotunda*

The above account of 1801 by a travelling clergyman tells of the 'Sabbath walks' laid out by Richard Reynolds, a Quaker partner in the Coalbrookdale works, who managed the company whilst Abraham Darby III was in his teens. Whilst it is still possible to trace the path to the Rotunda, much of Reynolds' splendid work has disappeared in the undergrowth.

The town of Ironbridge became a thriving community

LEFT: *Eighteenth-century Caughley 'mask' jugs depicting the Iron Bridge*

in the late eighteenth century and by the nineteenth century had been visited by many well-known people, including John Wesley and Benjamin Disraeli. Maori princes were sent to learn about iron-working, Italian and Polish nobility, Swedish and German engineers, industrial spies from France, clergymen, writers and artists all marvelled at the sights. Some were struck by the horror of it all, others by the beauty of the surrounding landscape which persisted despite the sulphur and lead. The Bridge itself became the inspiration for all kinds of

artistic endeavour and was found on snuff-boxes, porcelain jugs, cast-iron fireplaces, letterheads and trade tokens. Today it is still used as the logo for numerous companies and is as popular as ever.

In the twentieth century the town declined, shops and industries closed down, and only the New Town development of Telford rescued it. One enduring industry has thrived since establishing itself in the Gorge in 1931: the Merrythought Teddy Bear factory exports its soft toys worldwide.

ABOVE: *Nineteenth-century photograph of what is now the Museum's shop in the Square, adjacent to the Iron Bridge*

LEFT: *Harry Rogers, a well-known coracle-maker, paddling along the wharfage in the floods of 1946. The Cooperative Store on the right is now the Tourist Information Centre and Museum Offices*

RIGHT: *Celebrated Merrythought teddy bears made in Ironbridge*

Blists Hill

This is an unusual name for what has become one of Britain's best-known open air museums. Called variously 'Blesses' and 'Blisses Hill' in the past, Blists Hill was once a successful eighteenth-century 'industrial estate'. Today a small town has been created here with rebuilt cottages and workshops, crafts and trades, and a wealth of events which reflect life at the end of the nineteenth century.

Coal was mined here from the 1750s, and three decades later the rapid growth of the canal system linked the area to other industrial areas. To connect the Shropshire Canal down the sleep slope to Coalport and from there to the River Severn, William Reynolds completed his great engineering leap of the imagination, the revolutionary Hay Inclined Plane, in 1792. Visitors can still climb its steep gradient today, sometimes wishing they had been contented with the view alone but always amazed by its technical audacity.

Later the Blists Hill blast furnaces were built, producing the iron that was used in the forges and foundries of the valley to make the typical goods on which Britain's reputation as 'the workshop of the world' depended. Cast-iron window-frames, door lintels, cooking-pots and ranges great and small, and fireplaces both humble and grand for cottage or castle, locomotives and smoothing-irons – nothing was too great or too small for mighty iron.

ABOVE: *The Photographer's Shop, where visitors too can dress in costume of the period*

LEFT: *Cast-iron columns at the entrance – originally from a Victorian sewage works in Leamington Spa*

BELOW: *The real thing – Madeley High Street in 1890, where children have gathered to watch the unfamiliar activities of the photographer*

LEFT: *Blists Hill Open Air Museum – morning bustle outside the Candlemaker's. Can museums ever truly re-create the past?*

ABOVE: *Hand-painted landscape with jewelled surround on Coalport china*

LEFT: *Miners' Walk at Blists Hill*

BELOW: *Turn-of-the-century Craven Dunnill tile on display at the Jackfield Tile Museum*

BOTTOM: *Compare the words of children a century ago with the smiling faces of young visitors today*

'I went to work about eight years of age. I went to carry stones on top of the bank. I had 6d a day. It is heavy work to carry the ironstone, I was always very tired at night… I was two years at this work. They were all girls on the bank, except myself and another; six girls and two lads, the girls were tired at night… so many had so much to do.'

Blists Hill was in decline. The blast furnaces were blown out in 1912, but the brick works and mines clung on until World War II.

In the post-war years Blists Hill sank into dereliction, leaving a mass of tangled plateway and other abandoned remains of a once thriving centre of industry.

In the 1960s the creation of Telford New Town brought a massive injection of money into the East Shropshire Coalfield and the dawning realisation of the importance of many of its industrial relics.

Blists Hill opened to the public as a museum in 1973 with just a handful of exhibits. Its visitors were often enthusiasts of 'industrial archaeology' – then a new history specialism. Today visitors both young and old, specialists and tourists alike, all enjoy the qualities that ensure everyone finds their own meaning in Blists Hill.

ABOVE: *The chemist was a cheap alternative to the doctor in the 1800s*

RIGHT: *Supper for the porcine resident of Shelton Tollhouse. Many cottagers kept a pig and their own vegetable plot*

Besides coal, both clay and ironstone were extracted from the area. Hundreds of men, women and children worked long hours from early in the morning, picking over the iron ore and the coal heaps. Later the huge Brick & Tile Works, which covered most of the present-day 'upper town' of Blists Hill, provided employment for local people for well over a century.

The coming of the railways killed the short-lived canal mania in Britain. As competition increased, industry in Victorian Britain had to invest to succeed, but not all the industries in the Ironbridge Gorge understood this. By the end of the century

LEFT: *Traditional fairground in front of the blast furnace remains*

RIGHT: *The winding engine at the Blists Hill mine, once going down 700ft (213m)*

Blists Hill covers some 50 acres (20ha) of the former Madeley Wood Mining Company and Brick & Tile Works. Original features still remain, such as a section of the Shropshire Canal leading to the Hay Inclined Plane, Lee Dingle Bridge, which is a wrought-iron structure built to carry plateway track, and, of course, the Brick & Tile Works, of which some parts have been partially restored.

The Plumbers & Tinsmith are housed within some of the nineteenth-century former drying-sheds of the Brick Works, and the Blists Hill blast furnaces form the backdrop on the 'lower green' to the many summer events that enliven the town, such as historic travelling fairs and markets.

One of the most well-known local landmarks in the nineteenth century and during much of the twentieth was the Forest Glen, a refreshment pavilion built in 1889 on the slopes of the Wrekin hill, some 5 miles (8km) away. Visiting the Wrekin has always been a popular excursion for many Midlanders, who were sad to see the near destruction of this watering-hole in the early 1980s. The Museum Trust was fortunate to salvage the earliest section of the Forest Glen and rebuild it at Blists Hill, where it continues to fulfil its original role.

ABOVE & RIGHT: *The fame of the Forest Glen, built and owned by the Pointon family, ensured that it featured on Coalport pieces. Equally celebrated, however, was the collection of Coalport china which was formerly housed within the pavilion*

RIGHT: *A white hot bar of wrought-iron in the ironworks at Blists Hill, which is one of the only working examples in the world, employing equipment of the 1860s*

FAR RIGHT: *The plumber was a vital part of emerging domestic hygiene and sanitation in the nineteenth century*

Market Place (Market Day), Ironbr...

The local market had been at nearby Madeley since medieval times, but after the building of the Iron Bridge in 1779 and the subsequent growth of the eponymous town, the market was rapidly moved to Ironbridge (left) where it flourished until the 1980s – 'on market day, Friday and Saturday, the housewife would trudge to Ironbridge and go to her chosen dealer for bacon at 6d lb and fresh butter at 8d lb. Some dealers had cheese at 4d lb which was alive with maggots – reckoned by some to be tasty when toasted…'
DIARY OF CHARLES PESKIN

RIGHT: *The first female factory inspector in the area is known to have inspected the tile works at Jackfield in the 1920s. Not one to be trifled with, she may well have given Mr York, the Managing Director, a hard time over working conditions at Craven Dunnill*

BELOW: *Arthur Maw, Managing Director of the largest decorative tile works in the area, lived in Severn House, now the Valley Hotel. He decorated it with his company's products. Today guests can still enjoy some of their colourful and textured effects*

Jackfield

'The fag end of the world' was how Jackfield was once described! However, strangely enough, this unflattering description was applied by a man who then invested and established a most successful business in this small riverside settlement. Henry Powell Dunnill was a Yorkshireman who somehow saw the potential in this small village on the south bank of the Severn. Jackfield, at the eastern end of the Ironbridge Gorge, was crowded with the drinking-houses of the bargees and with small potteries that survived from decade to decade. Dunnill was not alone, and by the end of the century Jackfield was the home of the largest decorative tile producers in the world.

Maw & Co's Encaustic Tile Works was established here by George and Arthur Maw in the 1880s, having moved from their smaller site at Benthall, near the Iron Bridge. Craven Dunnill's factory was built in the early 1870s. Maw & Co's factory was three times larger than that of

Craven Dunnill, and the whole complex of tile works, dispatch yards, coal and clay, chimneys and kilns must have been an awesome sight.

quarters of a century, before finally succumbing to the decline of the Gorge and eventually closing in the twentieth century.

The Severn Valley Railway brought clays from Cornwall direct to the door of the two factories, and the design of the two tile works by Charles Lynam was based, for the first time, on the 'production line'. They flourished for three-

Tiles were fashionable and everywhere. Every colour and style, with patterns derived from nature and from geometry, were to be found in every sort of building, both at home and abroad. No bank or public house, no self-

respecting domestic hearth or hospital, railway station or public lavatory could be considered complete without appropriate tile panels. Maw & Co and Craven Dunnill supplied them worldwide, to Indian palaces, to banks in

North and South America, to South Africa and to Australia. It is hard nowadays to imagine that tiles from this little Shropshire village lined the walls of many international institutions.

ABOVE: *Craven Dunnill tile works in its heyday – an engraving from its first catalogue*

LEFT: *George Maw was a keen photographer and possibly took this picture showing other members of the family using the Meadow Ferry*

BELOW: *George and Arthur Maw successfully upgraded their operation over three decades*

⬧ MAW & C° BENTHALL WORKS ⬧
WORCESTER ⬧ 1850 ⬧ BENTHALL ⬧ 1852 ⬧ REBUILT ⬧ 1883

Life for the families of the owners of the tile works would have been comfortable and ordered. Amy, the daughter of Henry Dunnill, reveals some glimpses of her family life from her notebook:

'Sunday morning service at the Independent or Congregational Chapel began at 11.00 am … the congregation consisted entirely of working class people, except ourselves and Mr George Maw who with his brother, Mr Arthur Maw, owned the encaustic tile works at Benthall before their new premises were built at Jackfield …'

However, not everything was so simple:

'One of father's eccentricities was to have a cold tub every morning in a round portable bath, and I was brought up to enjoy the same bracing

LEFT: *Jug made free for the Half Moon public house on the understanding that it would be filled with beer free of charge!*

ABOVE: *Japanese image on an 1870's Maw & Co tile reflecting the contemporary passion for the oriental*

LEFT: *'Water Babies' designed by Walter Crane and made by Maw & Co in the 1890s*

ABOVE: *Tile-covered interior of Jackfield church*

LEFT: *A typically fine and detailed drawing by John Bradburn, who produced designs for many public buildings. He studied at the Coalbrookdale School of Art and returned to be Maw & Co's head of Architectural Faience before World War I*

experience. A very early recollection is of a winter morning, when the ice had to be broken in the bedroom water jugs, and Mama decided it was too cold for me to start my day as I usually did. I exasperated … "Very well, if you are such a naughty girl, you shall have your cold bath to punish you.'"

Many in the Jackfield workforce travelled by ferry from Coalport every day. Not until 1909 was the Haynes Memorial Bridge built. Never known by this name but always as the 'Free Bridge' because it was toll free, this was demolished in 1994.

Life was hard in most industries in the nine-teenth and early twentieth centuries. To modern eyes working practices involved physical drudgery, little or no hygiene, and rudimentary safety. Yet many of these factories were 'state of the art' by contemporary standards. Craven Dunnill and Maw & Co

were the best-known and the largest employers in Jackfield, but there were many other potteries, brick and tile works, all producing large volumes of materials for the building trades. Nearby Broseley, long famed for its roofing-tiles, was also one of the most

important centres for clay tobacco-pipe production.

Looking at the quiet village of Jackfield today, a high degree of imagination is required to understand just how tumultuous it must have been at the height of its manufacturing life.

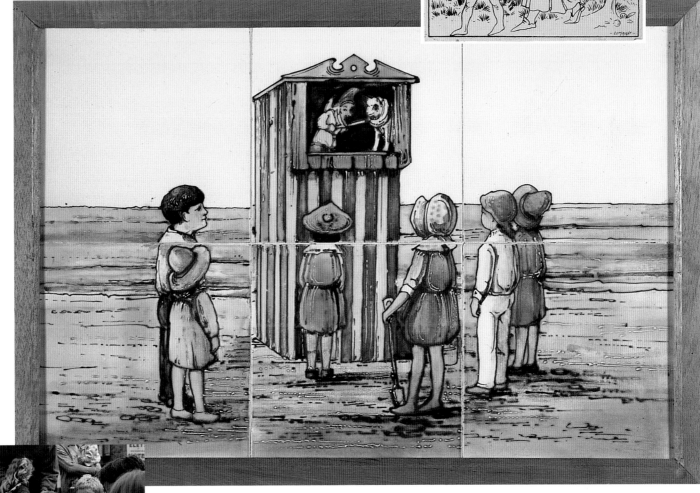

ABOVE: *Punch and Judy tile panel made by Maw & Co in the 1920s*

LEFT: *'Professor' Magor, a popular Punch and Judy entertainer at Blists Hill*

TOP RIGHT: *'Summer' – a Craven Dunnill tile of the 1870s from the 'Seasons' set*

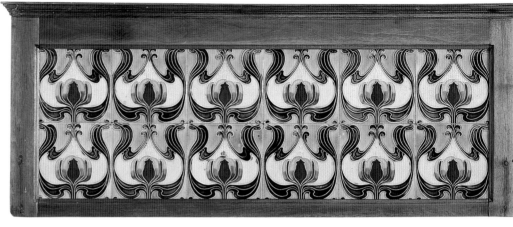

ABOVE: *A blockprinted geometric tile with gold finish, by Maw & Co from the early 1880s*

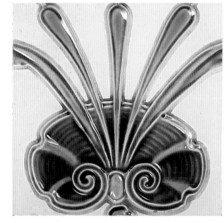

RIGHT: *Typical late Victorian moulded fire-place tile*

BELOW RIGHT: *Ruby lustre owls, inspired by William de Morgan. Craven Dunnill, 1890s*

LEFT: *Late Victorian 'charger', produced as part of Craven Dunnill's art pottery range*

The design of tiles was almost exclusively a highly respected male preserve. The School of Art based in the Coalbrook-dale Literary and Scientific Institution – now a youth hostel – thrived in the mid-nineteenth century and nurtured local design talent. Its success is reflected not only in tile designs but also in the decorative art castings made by the Coalbrookdale Company.

The art departments in the tile companies were well regarded, and in the Craven Dunnill factory theirs was adjacent to the trade show-room. The far distant part of the yard where the clay was delivered and left to 'weather' in the arcs outside was the domain of the unskilled end of the workforce.

Victorian tiles were first made from clay still in its malleable, plastic form. In the 1840s, however, a new technique was patented, which allowed tiles to be made from clay in 'dust' form. This speeded up the process considerably. Dust-pressing is

ABOVE: *An example of a standard wash-stand splash-back produced in their thousands before the First World War*

BELOW: *Floral inspiration*

still demonstrated at the Jackfield Tile Museum today.

At the turn of the century Craven Dunnill employed just 95 workers, considerably less than the 300 employees of Maw & Co.

After World War I the economic depression made survival hard for all decorative

ceramic industries. Across the river, Coalport never recovered, and Craven Dunnill gradually sank into decline, finally quitting manufacturing altogether after the Second World War.

Maw & Co limped on until 1970; its former works have now been converted into craft workshops and residential accommodation. In 1983 the Ironbridge Gorge Museum bought the semi-derelict Craven Dunnill premises, used latterly as a foundry, and opened up a small section to visitors one year later. Over subsequent years restoration has continued to show visitors the former glories of this once great producer of some of the most beautiful tiles ever made. Tile-decorating workshops, a geology gallery, ever-changing exhibitions and a tempting tile shop make this Museum deservedly popular.

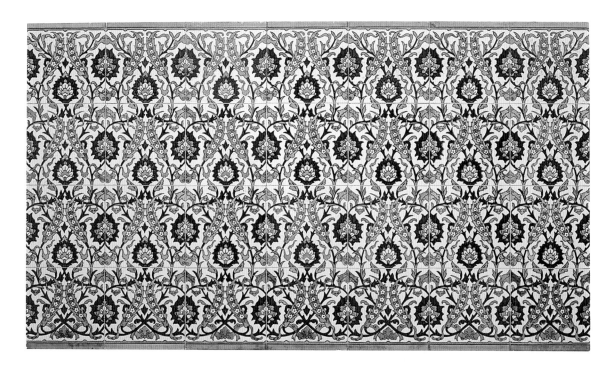

ABOVE: *Panels inspired by Persian designs were often used in public baths; this one by Maw & Co is from the 1880s*

BELOW & RIGHT: *Broseley, near Jackfield, had long been famous for its clay-pipes. The factory at Legges Hill was run by the Southorn family until the 1920s. Production at the King Street pipeworks lasted until the 1950s, when the works were abandoned and left untouched until acquired in the early 1990s to be interpreted as the Broseley Clay Tobacco Pipe Museum. In its heyday 50,000 pipes a week would have been fired in its kiln*

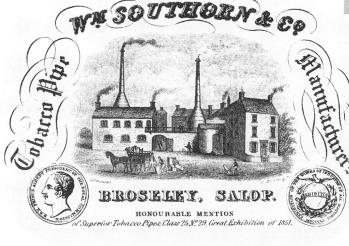

ABOVE: *Behind the scenes Jackfield Tile Museum cares for over 40,000 original patterns, moulds and tiles. The collection continues to grow and new displays are planned*

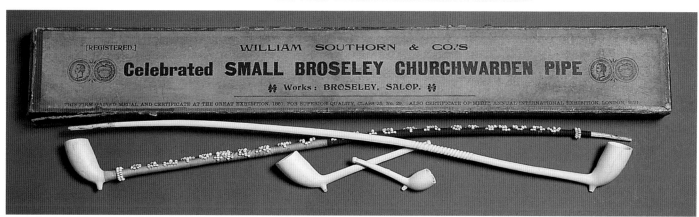

Coalbrookdale

Coalbrookdale today still contains many ironmasters' homes. Some remain private residences, others are now open to visitors, restored and maintained by the Ironbridge Gorge Museum Trust. Carpenters Row is still partially lived in, and reflects the style of workers' housing built by the Coalbrookdale Company. Some survive, others were demolished this century. The most prominent of the ironmasters' houses are those built on the hill above the Darby Furnace: Dale House, Rosehill, the Chestnuts, Sunniside and the White House, of which Dale House and Rosehill may be visited. The White House and Sunniside are long gone. Rosehill contains items that belonged to the Darby family, including furnishings, personal papers, clothes, books and Quaker history, creating a picture of the families who worked in the Dale for nearly 200 years.

RIGHT: Modern Coalport figurines reflect a predilection for costumes of the eighteenth and nineteenth centuries, far removed from the plain dress of ironmaster and worker alike

ABOVE: *Domestic necessities in Rosehill*

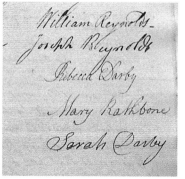

LEFT: *Quaker signatories on the marriage certificate of Abraham Darby III*

RIGHT: *1820s hand-painted, gilded teacup, from Coalport*

Slowly
Thy kingdom comes

the art and mystery
of casting and moulding
of Iron Potts

after weeks of trial
with the keyhole stopped

Barr Iron
for the forges
from Pit Coal pigs

after 6 days and nights
on the bridge of the furnace

Fire engine cillinders
cast iron rails
an Iron Bridge

all from the refusal
of Friends

plain Friends
to turn cannon.

FROM 'THE METAL OF MARS'
IN ROGER GARFITT'S
BORDER SONGS

MAIN PICTURE: *In 1800 Sarah Darby, sister of Abraham III, played a vital role in the management of the Coalbrookdale Company. A woman of determination, she ran the company together with manager Richard Dearman. She is imagined here in the study at Rosehill, then known as The Grange, where Dearman lived from 1791 until his death in 1804*

RIGHT: *Representations from life were commonplace. The deerhound table stands in the Glynwed Gallery in the Museum of Iron, where items from the Elton Collection include china, paintings, cartoons and art castings*

When the Coalbrookdale iron companies began to feel the effects of stiff competition from elsewhere in the country and the impending decline of business, this could have spelled the end of a short-lived success story. Instead, Francis Darby, son of Abraham III, spotted the Continental trend for art castings and propelled the company into decorative cast-iron. In 1834 the Coalbrookdale Foundry produced its first sculptures,

LEFT & ABOVE: *A beam engine from Lightmoor, near Coalbrookdale, which was dismantled in 1929 and shipped to the Henry Ford Museum in America. It came home in 1993, was restored by Ford UK, and is now in the Museum's 'Iron Mighty' collection, in working order*

plaques, candlesticks and other ornamental objects. In the middle of the nineteenth century the Coalbrookdale Foundry became the largest in the world. Its product range expanded, and its designers ensured that Coalbrookdale art castings were sought after internationally. The name of Coalbrookdale became the benchmark for superb fountains, gates, garden furniture, railings and lamps.

The culmination of this was the Great Exhibition of All Nations of 1851 in Hyde Park, which Francis Darby was fated not to see, having died suddenly the year before. The great entrance gates to the Exhibition were made here, later placed in Kensington Gardens where they still stand. The 'Boy and Swan' fountain designed by John Bell was displayed there, and is now restored and

ABOVE: *'Water for drinking and cooking all had to be carried … down the Dale in pails, cans and buckets from the Bathwell pump near the Viaduct pool … here was also a pump just inside the Upper Works which the manager allowed to be used by water carriers …' This picture shows the Bath Spout at Doseley*

ABOVE: *'Boy and Swan' fountain, Museum of Iron*

LEFT: *John Bell's fountain in the Great Exhibition catalogue, with the Coalbrookdale Gate in the background*

re-instated at the Museum of Iron.

The Great Warehouse was built in 1838. Its clock tower, added five years later, was perhaps an 'in-house' acknow-ledgement to Brunel's *Great Western*, the first transatlantic steamship, for in 1843 the Coalbrookdale company provided the ship's stoves.

This building is now the Museum of Iron, interpreting not only the beginnings of industry here but also the way of life of the people who worked in the iron industry for over 200 years.

RIGHT: *A working model of the world's first steam railway locomotive, made in Coalbrookdale in 1802. There is also a full-size working replica of Richard Trevithick's invention in the Museum's collection*

RIGHT: *The 'Eagle Slayer' by John Bell was displayed at the 1851 Great Exhibition. A smaller version is now in the Museum of Iron*

In 1823 a clergyman wrote an instructive pamphlet for 'Little-tarry-at-Home-Travellers': 'Driving down into Colebrook in the dusk of the evening is rather awful. The number of furnaces vomiting out flames and smoke make a prospect quite new, but not quite pleasant …'

In fact, far from being new, the furnaces of Coalbrookdale were by then already in decline.

The Museum of Iron contains not only some superb examples of Coalbrookdale decorative iron and bronze castings but it also shows how and why the valley grew to be the most heavily industrialised area in the world for a short time in the eighteenth century, before decline set in. The landscape of today hides many of its original features but is still redolent of the atmosphere of early industry. Glynwed's modern

The Forge
All I know is a door into the dark.
Outside, old axles and iron hoops rusting;
Inside, the hammered anvil's short-pitched ring,
The unpredictable fantail of sparks
Or hiss when a new shoe toughens in water.
The anvil must be somewhere in the centre,
Horned as a unicorn, at one end square,
Set there immoveable: an altar
Where he expends himself in shape and music.
Sometimes, leather-aproned, hairs in his nose,
He leans out on the jamb, recalls a clatter
Of hoofs where traffic is flashing in rows;
Then grunts and goes in, with a slam and flick
To beat real iron out, to work the bellows.
                                    SEAMUS HEANEY

ABOVE: *The Royal Society presented a gold medal to Abraham Darby III in 1787*

foundry behind the Museum of Iron still remains as testimony to the lasting skills of those early ironmasters, making Aga cookers, the natural descendant of Darby's original cooking-pots.

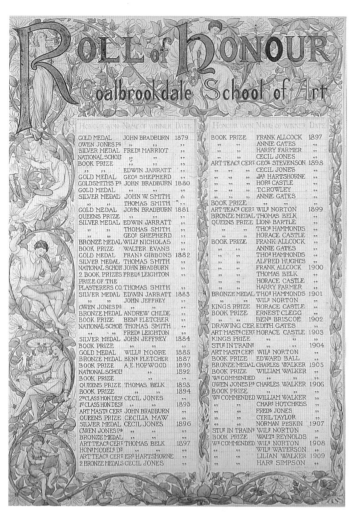

ROLL of HONOUR
Coalbrookdale School of Art

Honour won	Name of winner	Date		Honour won	Name of winner	Date
GOLD MEDAL	JOHN BRADBURN	1879		BOOK PRIZE	FRANK ALLCOCK	1897
OWEN JONES Pᶻ	"	"		"	ANNIE GATES	"
SILVER MEDAL	FREDᵏ MARRIOT	"		"	HARRY FARMER	"
NATIONAL SCHOLᵏ		"		"	CECIL JONES	"
BOOK PRIZE		"		ART TEACᵏ CERᵏ	GEOᵏ STEVENSON	1898
"	EDWIN JARRATT	"		"	CECIL JONES	"
GOLD MEDAL	GEOᵏ SHEPHERD	"		"	Aᵏ HARTSHORNE	"
GOLDSMITHS Pᶻ	JOHN BRADBURN	1880		"	HORᵏ CASTLE	"
GOLD MEDAL	"	"		"	T.C.ROWLEY	"
SILVER MEDAL	JOHN W. SMITH	"		"	ANNIE GATES	"
"	THOMAS SMITH	"		BOOK PRIZE		"
GOLD MEDAL	JOHN BRADBURN	1881		ART TEACᵏ CERᵏ	WILᵏ NORTON	1899
QUEENS PRIZE		"		BRONZE MEDAL	THOMAS BELK	"
SILVER MEDAL	EDWIN JARRATT	"		QUEENS PRIZE	LIONᵏ BARTLE	"
"	THOMAS SMITH	"		"	THOᵏ HAMMONDS	"
"	GEOᵏ SHEPHERD	"		"	HORACE CASTLE	"
BRONZE MEDAL	WILᵏ NICHOLAS	"		BOOK PRIZE	FRANK ALLCOCK	"
BOOK PRIZE	WALTER EVANS	"		"	ANNIE GATES	"
GOLD MEDAL	FRANᵏ GIBBONS	1882		"	THOᵏ HAMMONDS	"
SILVER MEDAL	THOMAS SMITH	"		"	ALFRED HUGHES	"
NATIONAL SCHOLᵏ	JOHN BRADBURN	"		"	FRANK ALLCOCK	1900
2. BOOK PRIZES	FREDᵏ LEIGHTON	"		"	THOMAS BELK	"
PRIZE OF THE PLASTERERS CO	THOMAS SMITH			"	HORACE CASTLE	"
SILVER MEDAL	EDWIN JARRATT	1883		"	HARRY FARMER	"
"	JOHN JEFFREY	"		BRONZE MEDAL	THOᵏ HAMMONDS	1901
OWEN JONES Pᶻ		"		"	WILᵏ NORTON	"
BRONZE MEDAL	ANDREW CHILDE	"		KINGS PRIZE	HORACE CASTLE	"
BOOK PRIZE	BENᵏ FLETCHER	"		BOOK PRIZE	ERNEST CLEGG	"
NATIONAL SCHOLᵏ	THOMAS SMITH	"		"	BENᵏ BRISCOE	1902
"	FREDᵏ LEIGHTON	"		DRAWING CERᵏ	EDITH GATES	"
SILVER MEDAL	JOHN JEFFREY	1884		ART MASTᵏ CERᵏ	HORACE CASTLE	1903
BOOK PRIZE		"		KINGS PRIZE		"
GOLD MEDAL	WILᵏ MOORE	1885		STUᵏ IN TRAINᵏ		1904
BRONZE MEDAL	BENᵏ FLETCHER	1887		ART MASTᵏ CERᵏ	WILᵏ NORTON	"
BOOK PRIZE	A.E. HOPWOOD	1890		BOOK PRIZE	EDWARD BALL	"
NATIONAL SCHOLᵏ		1892		BRONZE MEDAL	CHARLES WALKER	1905
BOOK PRIZE				BOOK PRIZE	WILLIAM WALKER	"
QUEENS PRIZE	THOMAS BELK	1893		OWEN JONES Pᶻ	CHARLES WALKER	1906
BOOK PRIZE		1894		Wᵏ COMMENDED	WILLIAM WALKER	"
2ᵏᵈ CLASS HONᵏDESᵏ	CECIL JONES	"		"	CHARᵏ HOTCHKISS	"
1ᵏ CLASS HONᵏDESᵏ		1895		"	FREDᵏ JONES	"
ART MASTᵏ CERᵏ	JOHN BRADBURN	"		"	CYRIL TAYLOR	"
QUEENS PRIZE	CECILIA MAW	"		"	NORMAN PESKIN	1907
SILVER MEDAL	CECIL JONES	1896		STUᵏ IN TRAINᵏ	WILᵏ NORTON	"
OWEN JONES Pᶻ		"		BOOK PRIZE	WALTᵏ REYNOLDS	"
BRONZE MEDAL		"		Wᵏ COMMENDED	WILᵏ NORTON	1908
ARTᵏTEACᵏ CERᵏ		"		"	WILᵏ WATERSON	"
HONᵏMODELS Dᵏ	THOMAS BELK	1897		"	LILIAN WALKER	1909
ARTᵏTEACᵏ CERᵏ	Eᵏᵏ HARTSHORNE	"		"	HARᵏ SIMPSON	"
2.BRONZE MEDALS	CECIL JONES	"				

ABOVE: *Coalbrookdale School of Art Roll of Honour, Jackfield Tile Museum*

RIGHT: *The Ironbridge Youth Hostel housed in the former Coalbrookdale Literary & Scientific Institution built by the Coalbrookdale Co in 1859*

CENTRE: *Inside the Museum Library*

the original papers relating to the building of the Iron Bridge. Students come here from all over the world to study, and the Museum works in partnership with Birmingham University to offer postgraduate courses at the Ironbridge Institute. Educational traditions that began in the mid-nineteenth century still continue today, and the whole of the Ironbridge Gorge is, in a sense, one giant classroom for anyone prepared to spend a little time here.

Over a century ago fine arts thrived next to heavy engineering. Craftsmen and women are once again flourishing in the valley, producing pottery, stained glass, decorative ironwork, cabinetwork and beautiful tiles, often housed within historic Museum buildings.

The history of Ironbridge is everyone's history. What happened here affected us all and irrevocably altered a way of life that had been unchanged for centuries. Railways, skyscrapers, cars and mechanisation all became much more possible because of the innovations in the Ironbridge Gorge over two centuries ago. It is for you, the visitor, to judge the results for yourself.

Museums reveal the results of much dedicated study and research but cannot show what happens behind the scenes. The Museum Library and Archives contain unique collections of books, photographs and documents, which include, for example, many of

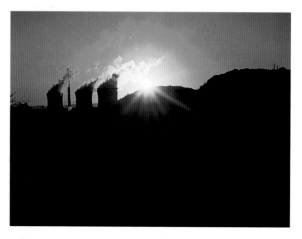

We changed into Victorian clothes for the school,
Left, right, left, right, the teacher said to us all.
The boys took off their caps and put them under their desk;
Outside we could hear the birds sing in their nests.

The girls gave a curtsy, the boys gave a bow,
The teacher said, 'Clean your nails right now'.
We sang a hymn, then said a prayer,
We sat on benches, the teacher sat on a chair.

When the class had ended we marched up a hill,
We then had a photo, we had to be still.
'Now go and get changed,' Mrs Cooper did call;
That was the end of our day at the school.

LEFT: *Sunset over the Ironbridge Power Station at Buildwas. Love them or hate them, these cooling towers represent the continuing generation of power in this valley*